MY GRAY WHALE
MIGRATION JOURNEY

BY JAMEE-MARIE EDWARDS   ILLUSTRATED BY PAULA ZORITE

PICTURE WINDOW BOOKS
a capstone imprint

Published by Picture Window Books, an imprint of Capstone
1710 Roe Crest Drive, North Mankato, Minnesota 56003
capstonepub.com

Copyright © 2025 by Capstone. All rights reserved. No part of this publication may be reproduced in whole or in part, or stored in a retrieval system, or transmitted in any form or by any means, electronic, mechanical, photocopying, recording, or otherwise, without written permission of the publisher.

Library of Congress Cataloging-in-Publication Data is available on the Library of Congress website.

ISBN: 9780756585389 (hardcover)
ISBN: 9780756585648 (paperback)
ISBN: 9780756585655 (ebook PDF)

Summary: Follow a gray whale on its magnificent migration journey.

Designer: Dina Her

Any additional websites and resources referenced in this book are not maintained, authorized, or sponsored by Capstone. All product and company names are trademarks™ or registered® trademarks of their respective holders.

Printed and bound in China. 6096

Greetings from the deep blue sea!

I am an Eastern North Pacific gray whale. I belong to the family of great whales.

Gray whales are some of the largest living animals on Earth. I can grow up to 49 feet (15 meters) long. That's the length of a large school bus. I weigh around 90,000 pounds (40,823 kilograms). That's as heavy as six large elephants.

Fun fact—I live in two different places. During the summer, I hang out in Alaskan waters. I spend most of my days showing off my **acrobatic** skills.

In the winter, I live off the coast of Mexico. Let me tell you all about my journey to Mexico!

I eat a LOT in the summer. Every day, I feast on 2,400 pounds (1,089 kg) of food. That's more than the weight of 500 bricks. Here's another fun fact—I eat lying on my side!

I find most of my meals at the bottom of the ocean. Small shrimplike creatures are my favorite. Yum! I will be traveling soon. I don't want to leave on an empty stomach.

In October, the Alaskan waters start to get cold. That's when my friends and I head for warmer weather. Thousands of us **migrate** to a place called Baja California. Despite its name, this area is in Mexico. I was born there eight years ago.

For some whales, this will be their first trip south.
It's the first of many trips they will take in their lifetimes.
Gray whales can live up to 60 years—sometimes more.

Baja California is a LONG way from Alaska. We travel at least 5,000 miles (8,047 kilometers) to get there. And we're pretty slow swimmers. At a top speed of 5 miles (8 km) per hour, it can take up to three months to reach it.

My friends and I travel in groups called **pods**. We swim during the day and at night. Scientists wonder how we sleep. Some think we can shut off parts of our brains and rest while we move. We have been spotted sleeping with one or both eyes open.

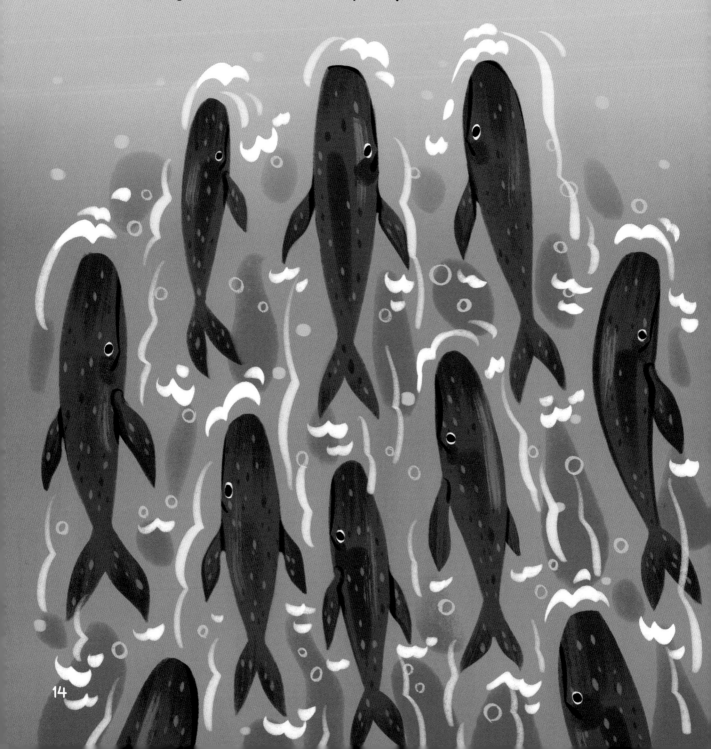

Scientists also wonder how we find our way to Mexico. Some think we look for familiar places when we peek our heads above water. This is called **spy-hopping**. Others think we use sounds to communicate with each other.

I swim close to the **shore** as I travel. When I come up to breathe, my breath forms a **spout**. It can reach up to 15 feet (4.6 m). My spout looks like a heart-shaped spray of water. Sometimes it makes a rainbow.

You'd think all that swimming would make us hungry. But nope! We filled up in Alaska. We don't eat much on our journey. We live off stored fat from all the food we ate there.

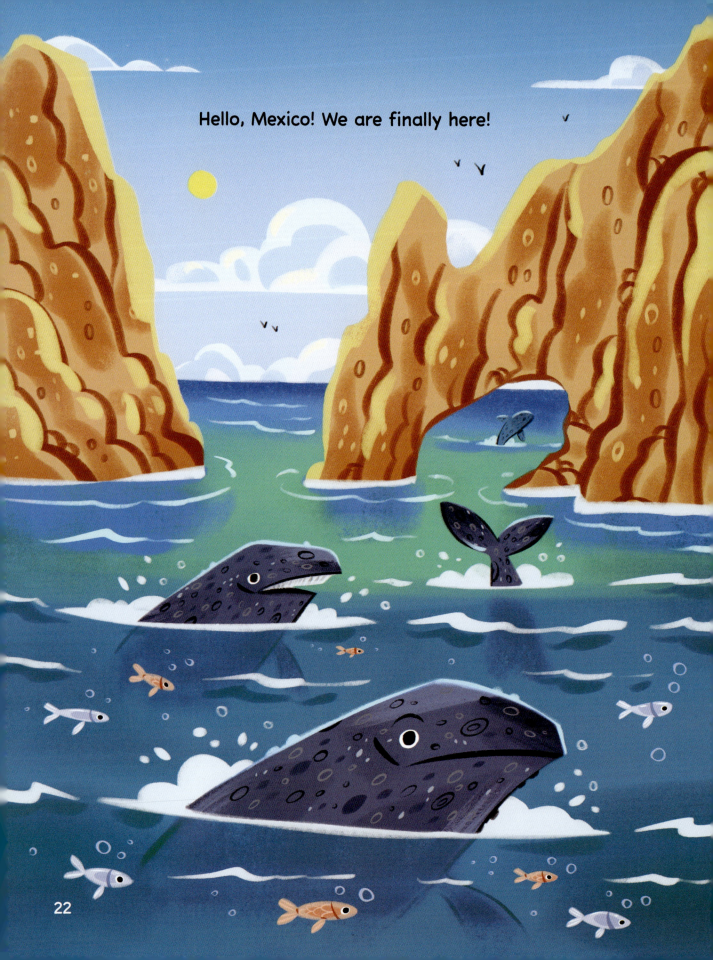

How do scientists know I am the same whale that began in Alaska? Look at my fin. Scientists placed a special tag on it. They can follow me wherever I go.

During the winter, my friends and I have fun in the warm Mexican waters. We are safe here. Local laws keep people from harming us.

Some whales find **mates** on the journey south. I met mine last year.

Baby whales are born here too. Gray whales grow inside their mommies for 12 to 13 months. A newborn gray whale is called a calf.

Surprise! I'm a new mommy. Meet my sweet calf.

By March, many whales have headed back north to Alaska. New mommies like me will stay another month or two. Our calves need to get stronger. They drink as much as 50 gallons (189 liters) of milk a day to fatten up for the journey.

Calves stay close to their mothers. Sometimes they swim onto their mother's back or tail **flukes**. When calves are strong enough, the rest of the whales begin the journey north. There, the **cycle** begins again.

ABOUT THE AUTHOR

Photo Credit: MaseFX

Jamee-Marie Edwards is an author, STEAM educator, and literacy advocate from New York City who is on a mission to ignite imagination and inspire children through creativity and education. Her experience in school health and health education has allowed her to connect with youth on various levels. As the founder of The Me I Need To Be Program, Jamee-Marie creates accessible platforms for learning in which she merges the arts and sciences to provide students with the opportunity to express themselves, build confidence, and gain essential skills. Learn more about Jamee-Marie at her website: maeinspireu.com.

ABOUT THE ILLUSTRATOR

Paula Zorite is a digital artist based in Valencia, Spain. She studied fine arts at the Polytechnic University of Valencia, where she discovered her passion for illustration. Paula has worked with a variety of authors and companies, creating vivid illustrations. Her style is characterized by a rich and harmonious use of color and a strong sense of narrative.

GLOSSARY

acrobatic (ak-ruh-BAT-ik)—movements similar to gymnastics, like handstands, flips, and forward rolls

cycle (SY-kuhl)—a set of events that happen over and over again

fluke (FLOOK)—a triangle-shaped half of a whale's tail

mate (MATE)—one of a pair who join together to produce young

migrate (MYE-grate)—to travel from one area to another on a regular basis

pod (POD)—a group of whales; pods range from less than five whales to more than 30 whales

shore (SHORE)—the place where the ocean meets land

spout (SPOWT)—a mist formed when a whale breathes out

spy-hop (SPYE-hop)—a whale behavior in which the whale pokes its head out of the water

INDEX

Alaska, 6, 10, 12, 20, 23, 28

breathing, 18

calves, 26, 27, 28, 29
communication, 16

eating, 8–9, 20, 28

laws, 24
lifespan, 11

mating, 25
Mexico, 7, 10, 12, 16, 22, 24
  Baja California, 10, 12

pods, 14

scientists, 14–15, 16, 23
size, 5
sleeping, 14
spouts, 18
spy-hopping, 16

tags, 23